ALEXINA
A WOMAN IN WARTIME YORK

BY
VAN C.M.WILSON

Published in Great Britain 1995.

Copies obtainable from :
V C Wilson
C/O 42 Frances Street
Fulford Road
York. YO1 4DP

Other titles by same author :
The History of a Community : Fulford Road District
of York. 1985

British Library Cataloguing in Publication Data
The Catalogue Record for this book is available from the
British Library
Wilson, Van 1995
Alexina, A Woman in Wartime York
Great Britain

ISBN No. 0 9525392 0 9

Price £3.50

CONTENTS

Preface

Acknowledgements

Chapter 1.   Early Days.   **1**

Chapter 2.   Bartons.   **16**

Chapter 3.   The A.T.S.   **25**

Chapter 4.   Back to York.   **33**

Chapter 5.   Endings and Beginnings.   **39**

Chapter 6.   Leo's War.   **43**

Chapter 7.   Leo and I.   **50**

PREFACE

What follows is a true story. Although it is written in the first person, it is not my story, but that told to me by Alexina herself. One or two of the names have been changed but all the characters and events are real.

I have tried where possible to verify dates, names and places, but as in all oral histories, there may be unavoidable errors, where the memory has played tricks.

ACKNOWLEDGEMENTS

I would like to thank the following people who have allowed me to quote from letters, supplied information and helped with verifying details in this book : Vivien Blaseby, Ivy Hutchinson, the late Ron Kerslake, Phyllis Lindsdell of the York Branch of the QMAAC, ATS & WRAC Association, Derek McTurk, Mary Poulton, and Rubye Readhead. I have also consulted the Yorkshire Evening Press at the Reference Library, and York City Archives for information on VE Day and Thanksgiving Sunday. I wish to thank Hugh Murray for allowing me to use some of his photographs of York in the 1930s, and Simon Hill for advice and for designing the cover.

I would like to thank Gill and Michael May and Margaret O'Donnell, for encouragement and positive comments about the manuscript.

Special thanks are due to three men who served with Leo in the RAF, who have given me detailed information, and made constructive suggestions. Amongst the group of Leo's friends whom I have met over the last few years, these three especially have taught me much about the RAF during the war, and about Leo himself, whom I never knew. I count it a privilege to be able now to call them my friends. They are Bill Foote (77 squadron pilot), Cyril Frazer (77 squadron wireless operator in India) and Bob Shields (Spitfire pilot with 66 squadron, who trained in Florida).

CHAPTER ONE
EARLY DAYS

When Neville Chamberlain made his fateful speech on Sunday 3rd September 1939, declaring that England was at war with Germany, we did not realise at first the gravity of the situation. The country had begun to prepare for war much earlier, and at school we were given demonstrations with gas masks, and had fire and air raid drills which we thought great fun, and a good excuse to get out of working. As well as the ordinary masks, we were also shown the infant respirators which completely enclosed the baby whilst its mother would pump in air with a handle.

If a German plane was sited, then the siren went and we would be marched into the shelter where we stayed until we heard the 'all clear.' If the siren sounded before twelve o'clock at night, we had to go to school next day, but if it was after midnight, then we had the following morning off to catch up on our sleep. If the 'all clear' did not sound for several hours, we were given the whole

Alexina, Derek and their mother

day off and were delighted. Although we felt a great sense of excitement, there was no indication that our lives would soon be changed forever. Everyone thought it would be over within a short time.

I left school at Christmas that year, just before my 14th birthday. There had been talk of raising the school-leaving age to 15, but this was suspended when war broke out. My brother Derek, who was 12, was still at the Model Elementary School for boys in Lord Mayor's Walk, which was attached to St John's Teacher Training College. By this time my father, who had been in France during the First World War, had been called up as a reservist and sent to Nantes, and I had to get a job to help with the family finances.

I started work as a junior at a gent's clothing outfitters. It was a long day, from nine to six during the week and nine to eight on Friday and Saturday. I was really just a skivvy, running everyone's errands, dusting and tidying up. The pay was 17/6 a week but there was no-one I could make friends with. The First Sales lived with the manager and was rather snooty. The only fun I had was with the tailor upstairs. I used to go up and talk to him, try on riding outfits and dinner jackets, and then he would let me have a go on the huge steam press.

Eventually, in July 1940, I left and went to work as Third Sales at Stead and Simpson's shoe-shop in High Ousegate. They also had a branch in Coney Street. I wasn't very keen on the plain brown dresses we had to wear and the hours were the same, with only half an hour for lunch (just time to eat our sandwiches in the back room), but the pay was 19 shillings a week plus commission of threepence in the pound, and the people were much pleasanter. We would have hundreds of shoes left out which had to be put away at the end of the day, and we always seemed to be busy, even though shoes were quite expensive, ranging from ten shillings to 25 shillings for the better quality ones. The wealthier customers always bought silk stockings whilst the rest bought rayon (there was no nylon yet). We could buy our own shoes at discount and artificial silk stockings for 1/7d.

The blackout was introduced in September 1939 and we had large black curtains covering the windows. Herald Printers in Coney Street sold sheets of black material for 3d and 6d but they soon ran out. Some people even bought

2

white paper and painted it black. The local ARP warden would come round to check that there was no light visible, and would warn us that if he saw any chinks, we could be in big trouble. Later we heard of people being fined up to 40s for showing light. We also had to criss-cross the windowpanes with masking tape to prevent them shattering. There were no street lamps and shop windows were no longer lit up, so we were always bumping into people and having to apologise, sometimes to lamp-posts. Car running boards and bumpers had to be painted white. At first we were not even allowed torches, though later we could use them if they were pointed downwards. But nothing happened - it was still the period of the 'phoney war.'

In the evenings we listened to the Home Service on the wireless. We loved Jack Buchanan's 'Songs from the Shows', the Billy Cotton Band Show and the Cocktail Cabaret, and quite often we would go out for a bag of chips at 9 o'clock, make a cup of Rowntrees cocoa and settle down to listen to a good play. Derek's favourite was Tommy Handley in 'Itma' (It's That Man Again) at 8.30 on Friday nights. The radio was an essential part of our lives. When we had lived in Nunnery Lane, in the early thirties, we had gas lighting and Derek would take the wireless accumulator (like a car battery, only made of glass, through which you could see the acid) to the corner cycle shop to be recharged. The wireless at Lumley Road worked from the mains electricity and was wired up to a loudspeaker so it could be heard in two rooms.

Sometimes I would go to the pictures with Mother or Derek. Our local cinema was the Clifton which had only opened in November 1937, the same year as the Regal in Piccadilly and the Odeon on Blossom Street. There were two foyers, one on the ground floor and one upstairs, and the cinema could seat over a thousand. It cost 6d for the front stalls, 9d for the middle and if you wanted the back rows or the circle, it would be a shilling. Before the main picture started, there was singing, accompanied by the large cinema-organ, and then the Pathe News which kept us up to date with events happening in the world. On Saturday nights and some Wednesdays we went to the Clifton Ballroom which was above the cinema. Tony Lister, the manager, would bring his record player and we danced to the big bands and swooned over the crooners. A few years later I heard Frank Sinatra, who became my favourite.

3

Give me Frankie's voice and the dancing of Fred Astaire and Ginger Rogers and I was in seventh heaven. As a child I went to tap dancing lessons, and in the mid-30s our group performed 'The Sun has got his Hat on' at the Joseph Rowntrees Theatre on Haxby Road, where I also did an impersonation of Jessie Matthews. I joined the Ovaltinies, and they transmitted 'secret messages' on the radio. We thought the code was ingenious, but it was only a series of numbers, each representing a letter of the alphabet. The message spelt out something like 'we love Ovaltine'!!

Clifton Cinema in 1995.

I met my first boyfriend, Larry, at the Clifton dance hall. He lived in Park Grove and was 18 and I let him think I was 16. We went to a few dances together until someone told him I was only 14. As he walked me home across the Croft to Lumley Road off Burton Stone Lane, where I lived, he sang, 'You broke my heart, 'cos you lied to me.' Then he kissed me on the cheek, murmured, 'Sorry kid' and was gone.

My best friend was called Connie. We had both been to Shipton Street school, where the headmistress was very strict and walked around swishing the cane, and we still spent a lot of time together, often going into the country on cycle rides. We would sometimes go to the Homestead Park at Water End, or shout for the ferry to take us across the Ouse to Poppleton Road. I was also friendly with a girl called Barbara but her parents were rather strict and would

4

not let her out very often. She was scared of her mother, who could be seen out looking for Barbara, on an ancient sit-up-and-beg bicycle.

Derek and I were 'pictures mad' and as well as the Clifton, we would often visit the Rialto, St George's, the Regal and the Tower. The cinemas (there were ten in York at that time) stayed open throughout the war except for a few days at the beginning when they were all closed by national order. When they did re-open, the hours were shorter but it would have been terrible if cinemas and theatres had remained closed. Together with dance-halls, they provided our main source of entertainment and escapism over the next six years.

Unfortunately, Derek had his bike stolen from the carpark at the Rialto on Fishergate and it was later found minus some parts near Fulford Barracks. He had it taken again in 1941 from outside the Model School, complete with gas mask in carrier bag. Next day he saw a young boy riding it along Lord Mayor's Walk. The boy had turned the handlebars around but Derek recognised it immediately, grabbed the kid and took him to the headmaster who sent for the police. Derek would have known that bike anywhere as he built it up from nothing when he was a paper boy in 1940. There was a court case and the boy was fined but Derek never got back his gas mask or dynamo.

We also enjoyed going to the Theatre Royal, where the plays were changed weekly. It was the same repertory company who performed in most of them and my favourites were Pauline Letts, who appeared right through the war, Raymond Francis and Michael Rennie who came in 1940. We usually sat in the circle or the orchestra stalls which were both 1/6. The cheapest seats were in the gallery, which only cost 4d. We always had to take gas masks with us and if there was an air raid warning, an announcement would be made giving the audience the choice whether to leave or remain. Once the doors were closed, the performance would resume. The nearest shelters were round the corner by the Public Library.

There were several public shelters in Clifton (the biggest at Bootham Grange) and others dotted all over the city. There were also some big trench shelters at Lord Mayor's Walk, the Library and Scarcroft Stray, which could hold several hundred people. Connie and I once took refuge in the shelters beneath the Bar Walls, a warren of dirty passages. Being pitch black in there, it

5

seemed worse than being outside. Some people had Morrison shelters inside their homes, which really resembled cages! You could put a cloth over the top and use it for a table, but it still looked rather an eyesore and took up half the room. Others might take a candle into the garden shed, but as the sheds were brick built, the shelter there wasn't really adequate. The Andersons were probably the safest, but the disadvantage was that so many of them would fill with water, which came up through the clay.

We spent quite a bit of time in the Anderson shelter in the garden of Lumley Road, which had nasturtiums growing above it. It was a sizeable garden, surrounded by bushes, and one side was covered in lupins. We had bought the semi-detached house when it was newly built in 1935, for the sum of 350 pounds. We had not been there very long when Derek was taken into the fever hospital with diptheria. He had to be carried to an ambulance at the end of the street because it had not yet been surfaced. Later we always used the Croft pathway at the bottom of the road, to cut through into Clifton. It brought us out next to Wilkins newsagents, and almost opposite Dandy's cake-shop.

At the end of Lumley Road was a school hockey field. The land was dug up and divided into allotments, as we were exhorted to 'Dig for Victory!' Dad was away so the man next door helped Derek to dig up a section and plant vegetables and potatoes in there.

Lumley Road today

6

By 1940 the war had begun in earnest. Bombs had dropped on Driffield and near Beningbrough about ten miles from York, so we wondered if we would be next. Sometimes we even slept in our clothes in case the siren went. Odd planes got through and dropped their loads on munition stores and factories. I remember my mother took her best coat to the cleaners and they sent it off to their factory in Liverpool which got bombed. She finally got some compensation much later. There were barrage balloons in various places and we would occasionally see one break free and go floating away before crashing to the ground.

On Sunday mornings Connie and I often went to play miniature golf by the riverside with three local boys from Archbishop Holgate's School. Another boy we were friendly with was Peter Stephenson who lived on the corner of The Avenue. He had been at Shipton Street then St Peter's School before joining up. We still saw him when he came home on leave. Many people seemed to go into uniform overnight and lots of boys I knew suddenly went away.

After five months in the shoe-shop it was time for another change, and I left to become an apprentice at Kathleen Benson's hairdressers in St Helen's Square, above Watkinson's boot and shoe shop, next to Barclays Bank Chambers. I would sweep up and wash hair, but never completed my training because when the receptionist left, I was given her job. One night a week I had to fire-watch. Two of us slept on camp-beds in the salon in case any flares were dropped. We had tin helmets and our equipment consisted of a stirrup pump, a bucket of water and two buckets of sand. The job was pretty boring, because most of the girls were older and had lots of boyfriends, which was their main topic of conversation. But I enjoyed the fire-watching. I also became an ARP messenger and would report to the control centre at the Guildhall. The passage on the right hand side of the main entrance led into offices, and the centre was down a flight of stairs, and partly underground. Many teenagers acted as messengers, delivering notes for the wardens to various places in the city. Once I went down Commonhall Lane beneath the Guildhall, which runs down to the riverside. In ancient times it was used to remove prisoners by boat, and its archway can still be seen from Lendal Bridge.

In 1941 clothes became rationed and utility garments were introduced bearing a special mark CC 41. The materials were satisfactory but a bare minimum of cloth was used, with no extras, and only a few buttons and seams. We got sick of hearing the phrase 'Make Do and Mend', which was the title of a threepenny government booklet, full of ideas and tips on how to make the best of the situation. If we wanted to wear anything fashionable, then we had to create it ourselves. We liked bright colours, which helped to raise our spirits when life seemed gloomy. My gran gave me her old ponyskin fur coat and I cut it up and made a bag and hat out of it, which lots of people admired. I would also wear plaid waistcoats, different coloured turbans and jumpers with different coloured sleeves to vary the few outfits I possessed. I had a little black hat which I edged with old squirrel fur and turned it up at the front, and I put a thick band of corduroy round another hat, and two large feathers in the brim. It was so tall that I had to bob down on buses. I made big bows out of old material and pinned them to the necks of white blouses, and it wasn't long before the trend caught on with other people. It was normal to swap items of clothing, to pass on what we had got tired of, and to beg something different from relatives and friends in exchange.

The other bane of our lives was food rationing which began in January 1940 and continued right up until 1954! It started with bacon, ham, sugar and butter, but gradually more and more things became rationed. We were sent leaflets about how to cope with the new ration books, but we never really got used to the endless queues for everything. The newspapers were full of recipes for such tempting meals as 'sardine and egg scramble' (without the fresh eggs!) 'sausage and bean pie' and 'oatmeal and mince'! Apparently you could even buy booklets telling you 1001 things to do with a potato! Our diets were really dreary, with dried eggs, whale meat, even horse meat! We might often have to wait for an hour hoping to get something appetising and then find there was none left! We were members of the Co-op (Co-operative Society) which operated like a club. Each time we bought something, we quoted our dividend number, and were able to claim back a percentage of what had been spent. We knew about the black market, where scarce goods were available....for a price. We passed on recipes and swapped coupons with neighbours and friends, and all believed in sharing what we had, however little it was.

In September 1941 I went to work at the North Riding Mental Hospital (the name was changed to Clifton Hospital in 1948) on Shipton Road, part of which had been requisitioned for about 500 military personnel. Auntie Dolly (Mum's eldest sister who lived with us), and my mother, ran the canteen and tuck shop there, so I helped them. I liked it much better as I got to meet lots of people in the forces, including the RAF boys in their glamorous blue uniforms. Dolly was in her element, just as she had been during the First World War, when she had helped to run the free canteen at the station for servicemen and women who were passing through. The WVS had started it up again at the beginning of this war. When we first went to the hospital canteen, we could hear a lot of noise coming from the kitchen, and thought there were about six men in there, clattering about and shouting at each other. Dolly told us to peep round the door, and we were amazed to see just two little men washing up. They were patients and the two of them were making all that racket!

For a woman it was very easy to get jobs. The newspapers were always full of situations vacant and there were usually several columns under the heading 'women workers.' I suppose I took it for granted that jobs were plentiful and as soon as I got bored, there were lots of other choices. My mother was quite amazed at this, because her own opportunities had always been so limited, and life was doubly constrained by having children. She had also had to live through the Depression when things were very bad. She told me that she envied the new freedom of younger unattached women. It was such a contrast to her own youth. Wartime brought with it a different way of life for women, but it wasn't always easy to adapt.

The hall at Centenary Methodist Chapel in St Saviourgate also became a forces canteen and we would go there some evenings with Dolly who went to the chapel regularly. When we were children, she had taken Derek and I there on Sunday evenings. She always kept a few toffees in her pocket and would get them out during the sermon, when Derek and I were poking and pulling faces at each other behind her back. After chapel she would give us each a bar of McEwans toffee. She did a lot for Centenary chapel, walking miles collecting

9

jumble, knitting and sewing and making jam and chutney for their annual Sale of Work each September. She dedicated her whole life to the chapel and to us, and lived with the family until she died. She never married, having lost her fiance in the Boer War in 1900. She was twenty years older than Mum, whose own mother had died when she was only one, so Dolly became a second mother to her nine brothers and sisters.

The canteen had started as a result of servicemen coming along on Sunday evenings after the service, for a cup of tea and a 'Singsong' in the schoolroom behind the church. They sang hymns, were given a talk and then usually finished by singing 'Abide with Me.' The 'Singsong' was later broadcast twice on the Home Service. The minister would give out New Testaments in khaki or Air Force blue covers. It was much more informal than the church itself, and they were allowed to smoke and drink tea in there.

The canteen opened on 25th September 1939 and was initially only open on one evening a week. Numbers steadily grew, until by 1940 servicewomen also started to come, and it stayed open every night of the week from about 6.30 to 11pm, as well as Saturday and Sunday afternoons. It was run by volunteers, the women of the church operating on a rota system, and the organisation was done by a committee of eight who were faced with a lot of paperwork, especially when it came to the food and the allocation of rations. While Dolly cooked or served, we would help out, and play table tennis and billiards. There were lots of games available, and a reading and writing room. Another aunt, Miriam, worked there too and she also invited soldiers to her home to have meals with the family. They were glad of this hospitality and, in return, would help with chores and even the children's homework.

There were two huts behind the church which were separated by shutters. The bigger hall was used for meals and on Wednesday nights there was a concert and up to 400 would come along to that. There were lots of local concert parties who appeared, and other groups from Leeds, Hull and Harrogate, as well as singers, musicians and comedians from ENSA. There was one local army band which often played in the early days and once or twice the 'Stars in Battledress' visited. On Tuesdays there was a social evening, and on Fridays it was film night. On ordinary nights, there would be about 200-300 congregating there. The ladies served food such as pork pies, spam, peas and chips and pilchard sandwiches, followed by slabs of cake, with tea and camp coffee to drink. One of the ladies told me that they could get 90 cups of tea from a quarter of a pound. The people from the chapel threw themselves into this work and obviously satisfied a great need. It was not just a place to eat, but somewhere to go to relax, meet people and have fun. At Christmas there was a big party and the canteen staff would put on a show. People came there from all over the world, and one night there was even a man with a flash on his coat which read 'Seychelles'! There was a regular Canadian who brought parcels to share out and so the ladies christened him Father Christmas. The servicemen were always full of fun and laughter, despite the fact that there was a war raging. It was easy sometimes to forget what was happening in the world, as nothing bad had touched us yet.

Centenary Methodist Chapel (Now Central Methodist Church), St Saviourgate

11

There were other canteens in the city including those at the Salvation Army and Wesley Chapel, Priory Street, but Centenary was the most central and probably the second most popular, after the NAAFI in St George's Field.

When I was 16, Connie and I started to go to dances at the Albany in Goodramgate, on Wednesday and Saturday nights. It was only 1/6 to get in. They held dances four nights a week, with Thursday as an 'old-time' night. The dances started at 8 o'clock, but many of the servicemen would go to the pub first and didn't come over before 9.30. We usually arrived quite early and then spent ages getting ready in the Ladies' cloakroom, which was upstairs. We would emerge looking our best, thinking we were the 'bees' knees'. I had to leave at 10.30 even though the dances didn't finish until 11pm.

Albany Hall, Goodramgate (Courtesy of Hugh Murray)

The dance-hall, which had begun as Miss Cooper's Dancing Academy, was next to Victoria Hall, once a cinema. Inside there was accommodation for 250, and there were mirrors all around, and a beautifully sprung floor, with the dance band in the corner. At the far end were doors leading through into a lounge filled with armchairs, and another door led into a smaller room where you could get coffee and sandwiches. It was there that Connie and I met a boy called Johnny Fazakelli from Liverpool who was stationed at Fulford Barracks, and we started getting invited up there for parties.

In 1942, Derek started work as an apprentice at Myers and Burnell of Davygate, the Standard and Rolls Royce garage and coachbuilders, and I began to work part-time for the Fire Service as a telephonist, one or two nights a week and occasionally at weekends. I still had my job at the hospital canteen so I must have had bags of energy.

It was April 1942 when we witnessed the Baedeker air raid on York. We were in the Anderson shelter for hours with the bombs raining down outside. Auntie Dolly was praying, Derek and I wanted to look out to see the action and Mother was more interested in going back into the house to get the bottle of whisky. The raid lasted most of the night and after it was over, we found all the windows broken and slates off the roof. In fact part of the roof had fallen in and had to be covered in tarpaulin, and oilcloth pinned on the windows. Later my mother claimed she had found a bullet in the bed. A bomb had dropped on the field behind Lumley Road and they said you could fit a double-decker bus into the hole it made. Earth and grass were thrown everywhere but it didn't explode.

Bootham and Clifton were in a dreadful state. The York City Supporters Club had been hit and the bottles were broken and spilt. Our old school, Shipton Street, had also been damaged. We walked up Burton Stone Lane and saw the rescue services digging out people and dead bodies. Men coming home after a night's work, made their way through the debris, terrified of what they might find. At these sights fear really began to overtake us and we had to struggle to fight it off. We seemed to suddenly grow up, having to face the fact that people we knew had died.

Yet we tried to laugh. Otherwise we would have gone mad. Connie's house in Crichton Avenue had been affected and bombs dropped over the road from her. There was no light as the electricity had failed. At 6 o'clock in the morning, I went round to the house. I couldn't believe what I was seeing. Both the front and back doors had been blown off in the blast, and there was only a hole where the local grocer's shop had once been, further down the street.

When there was no answer to my shout, I walked in, wondering if Connie was all right. She and her mother, who was eight months pregnant, were sitting in a corner covered in soot, with rubble nearby, where the chimney had collapsed. I was so shocked that I burst out laughing, and this broke the tense atmosphere. They stood up, looked at themselves in the mirror and began to laugh too. The numb feeling of terror and despair which had possessed them for most of the night, had begun to disappear. It was a few hours before her father, an air raid warden, returned home. He had been out all night attending the injured. Connie's cousin Betty, who worked with the Fire Service, was on duty that night. She was on the telephone, answering a call, when a bomb went off nearby and she was blown across the room, still with the phone in her hand, as the force tore it out of the wall.

Derek had a small cabin boat moored at Fulford, which he had bought for six pounds from a man going into the army. It was beached on the bank and when it flooded, he and Dad pushed it in and paddled it down to Clifton Ings. It kept drifting away so it was quite a hair-raising experience. Unfortunately, the boat was sunk in the air raid, with heavy rocks falling on it. Everyone was so relieved that Derek wasn't on it at the time.

On 26th May 1942, I joined the ATS after finally persuading my mother to let me go. Of course I was under age, but I told them I was 18. They didn't ask for my birth certificate, even though I had to fill in lots of forms and have a medical, and I found out there were lots of other girls who were too young to be there! Connie wanted to join up too but her mother refused, so she did her war work at Handley Page aircraft factory at Rawcliffe, repairing Halifax bombers, and became a fully qualified riveter. The planes were brought on trucks to the hangar, some spattered with blood, and in quite a mess. The workers patched shell holes along the bodywork, some small and some quite large. It was difficult to imagine how the aircrews had overcome these hazards, and of course some had not. Connie worked on the top with a rivet gun, and a young lad would be underneath holding the dolly, a piece of metal, just in his hands. It was a primitive process but they managed to make the repairs, so that the aircraft could fly again. They would also climb into the cockpits and scrub them out, trying not to think about what had happened to the occupants. Connie and I saw less of each other after that. She became involved with a serviceman, but he was shot down over the channel, and then suddenly a year later she had a letter from him. He was in a German POW camp, and she wrote back, but they eventually lost touch and never saw each other again. In May 1944, she married Don, an airman we'd met at the Albany in early 1942. We kept in touch but didn't meet again for several years, when Connie had become a young mother and returned from her travels abroad with Don, who remained in the RAF after the war.

After joining up and training at Pontefract, I was sent to Derby and boarded with a family who treated me horribly. They gave me hardly any food, in fact their idea of a good meal was a plate of carrots from their allotment. They had a monstrous little boy who went through my things when I was out, daubed my make-up everywhere and broke my compact mirror. I was sure he had pinched a couple of parcels Mum had sent, because I never got them. I was afraid to complain, being young and vulnerable, but I became more and more desperately homesick and eventually ran away back home.

I had been in the forces for only a short time, but I was home for two weeks before they missed me. By this time, Dad had returned from France with rheumatoid arthritis, and was in a hospital for a while down south. It plagued him until the end of his life and he always claimed that it had started at Dunkirk in 1941, being waist-deep in water for so many hours. When he found I had joined up he was angry and when I arrived home in a state, he played hell with the authorities. They were furious also, and I had to go back to get an official discharge on 12 December 1942, a humiliating experience. Yet both of us must have got over this, because two years later I joined up again and they took me without a qualm.

15

CHAPTER TWO
BARTONS

By the end of 1942, I was allowed to stay out later and would sometimes go in the Half Moon, the Punch Bowl in Stonegate, Thomas's in Museum Street and most often the Olde Starre. We got to know Walter and Irene who kept the Starre and it was one of the best pubs in York. It was always crowded in there. Coats were hung on the back of the door until they were inches thick. We knew a police inspector called Mike who went in there, and one night he was complaining that there was nowhere to put his coat. Someone said, 'Hang it on the door, Mike, it'll be all right.' An hour later he went to retrieve it and it had disappeared! There was another regular, a woman whose husband was away in the army. One night she came in and told us she had just got a letter from him, and said she would read some bits out. We wondered what on earth she was doing when she produced a toilet roll from the recesses of her handbag, until we realised that this was the letter.

The night-watchman at Grisdale's outfitters in Coney Street, (well-known for their 'Grisdale waterproof mac') often went in the Starre. He was supposed to be caretaking and fire-watching but would nip out for a drink and end up staying all evening. If you wanted anything, this man could get it. My cousin Rubye's boyfriend bought her a fob watch from him, with a case in the shape of a heart. Rubye told me about another man called Willy who always had things to sell. He rented a house in Little Stonegate and had to look after a brood of children, after his wife died suddenly under the anaesthetic at the dentist whilst having some teeth out. One night Willy said he had something 'special' at his house, so a few people trooped round the corner and went in. There was a long passage with flagged floors and a room on the right, from which they could hear scraping and rustling sounds. When they asked what the noise was, he opened the door of the parlour to show them. The room was a big one, with no furniture, but in the centre stood an enormous horse! At the far side was the cart which went with it!

Occasionally we went to Betty's but I preferred to go there in a crowd. A woman going in alone might give off the wrong signals. Betty's Bar contained a mirror on which servicemen and women, but mainly aircrew, scratched their names. Another bar downstairs served food and there was also a restaurant upstairs. It was the forces' favourite and well-known all over the world. All nationalities went in there - Australians, Poles and Canadians as well as our own boys. People who had never been to York, or even to England, would arrange to meet up in Betty's Bar. It opened in 1936 along with Betty's in Harrogate. The owner Frederick Belmont had been that year on the maiden voyage of the Queen Mary. Consequently the ballroom was modelled exactly on the interior of that famous liner, in Art Deco design, with long mirrors and chandeliers. On the Queen Mary there was also a mirror where celebrities engraved their names.

Betty's in 1995

York pubs closed about 10pm so we would then go out to Fulford and Bishopthorpe where they stayed open until 10.30 or 11. Opening times did tend to vary though, because sometimes they ran out of beer or glasses. Some places might then only open for an hour, from 8 to 9, or from 9 to 10, closing when there were no drinks left. There would often be a notice saying 'Plenty of beer here' beside the V for Victory sign on the front door of the pub.

Then I met John, who was a Flight Lieutenant, very tall and good looking. He had a public-school accent and would take me out when he wasn't flying. With him I went to the theatre, to services at the Minster and afternoon tea at the Bide-a-Wee Cafe on Museum Street. We also went to the Picture House cinema and cafe in Coney Street. At one service in the Minster I wore a smart new grey coat with maroon hat and matching bag and gloves. I had some new shoes too but couldn't wear them because of blisters on my heels, so had to resort to sandals, which rather spoilt the effect! It was my new outfit for the year and had taken most of my coupons. At the beginning of the war we were allowed 66 coupons each year, but this was later reduced. Stockings alone took two coupons so they didn't go far.

One Tuesday I had arranged to meet John at the theatre but I got a message at the last minute to say that he was flying and couldn't make it. That was the last thing I heard. When I made enquiries I was just told that he was 'unavailable', until finally I realised that he had been killed. The boys would make jokes and laugh all the time to disguise their true feelings. If any of their friends 'bought it', they would go out and get very drunk.

Our local pub was the Burton Stone and that was always filled with airmen. I got to know the actor Pat (Patrick) Kinsella there who was also in the RAF. He would recite Shakespeare with a pint of beer balanced on his head, then stand up without spilling a drop. He was in the film 'Banana Ridge', a Ben Travers farce starring Robertson Hare. He played the dashing young cad, Jones, with the David Niven moustache, who finally gets the girl after a lot of misunderstandings over identity. Pat was killed in action in 1942 and the film didn't reach York until January 1943, when it came to the Regent in Acomb. Someone told me that his crew had taken a new wireless operator along on their last mission, and it was always considered bad luck for someone new to stand in. That night all the crew except the wireless op were killed.

At weekends we would bike out to Linton-on-Ouse for picnics there. Later we got invitations to parties at the officers' mess at Linton, Elvington, Full Sutton and Church Fenton. The latter was home to several fighter squadrons, some on Spitfires, some on Hurricanes and some on Mosquitoes. After 1943 there were two Polish squadrons stationed there. There would be a coach at Exhibition Square to pick up those with invitations at 7 o'clock, and it would bring us back from the camp at 1.30 in the morning, and drop everyone off near to where they lived. Canadian parties at Linton were the best because they could get food which was rationed to the English. The spread was always fabulous and the mess beautifully decorated. The Americans and Canadians earned two or three times as much as the British, and always seemed to have plenty of money. There were lots of Canadians in the RAF before they came en masse in their own RCAF squadrons in 1943.

The Burton Stone Inn today

Although petrol was rationed, many of the lads had cars, usually old jalopies, and four or five would pile in to come from the aerodromes into York. One boy, Allan Farrar, could get about ten in his jalopy, which was a converted hearse. I went in it a couple of times but preferred the comfort of a two-seater sports car. There were some boys who didn't have cars and they would get the bus in from Linton and the last bus back to camp about 1 a.m. If the dance didn't finish until late, they would put us in a taxi and pay for it before catching the bus themselves. A lot of the crews used bicycles, and one boy, Fred, who was in the Free French Air Force stationed at Elvington, had a ramshackle old bike with no brakes and no lights. He often came into York holding onto the back of a lorry. He had been in the Riffs, riding in the desert. Later I heard that he was shot down when Paris was liberated in 1944.

At the age of 16, I had become a member of the York Female Friendly Society. For a small regular payment, we qualified for sickness and maternity benefits, pensions and even death benefit. The assistant secretary of the York Branch was Joyce Bell. She was the daughter of Canon Bell of York Minster, and wrote plays. Her thriller 'The Woman in the Case' was broadcast on the BBC Home Service in January 1943.

Alexina in garden of Lumley Road

That same year I learned to drive with the British School of Motoring, four lessons at five shillings each. There were no tests and it was easy to get a driving licence. When war broke out, all provisional licences became full ones, if the driving was considered to be 'of national importance.' Then I went to work at G. E. Barton's catering and confectionery business where I stayed until 1944. The company was quite a large one (in fact Bartons and Terrys were the main catering firms in York), with the bakery occupying land on Bedern, near the old Bedern School which had closed in 1940. As well as shops in Goodramgate and Bootham, and the Tea Rooms in Piccadilly, there were also the Davy Hall Restaurant and the Tudor Cafe in Davygate. The head office in Bedern had once been the Manor Rooms dance hall, and the vans were parked in St Andrewgate near workshops and stores.

Derek was a mechanic at the garage in Ebor Buildings, off Aldwark, and Auntie Dolly was managing the shop in Bootham, almost opposite Grosvenor Terrace. Aunt Miriam worked as a caterer for special functions, such as race meetings and weddings, and dinners at the club on Lendal Bridge. The manager of Davy Hall was Percy Barton, son of G.E. himself, and he had once worked in the kitchens of Buckingham Palace. Percy (or Dick as everyone called him) would go round to Miriam's and ask her to get together a team of women for a particular event which was coming up. I started working for Bartons as a driver's mate helping Arthur Yates to load and unload. I did a bit of relief driving, and later accompanied a woman called Mary, before finally getting my own green van.

Davy Hall Restaurant, late 1920s. (Courtesy of Hugh Murray)

It was a funny little van and the starter used to jam so you had to lift the floorboards up beside the passenger seat and just loosen it. Once it stalled at Micklegate traffic lights and I had to get out, with all the cars behind hooting at me, and release it with a spanner. I got it going and got to Boston Spa and it broke down again, and the spanner wouldn't work it so I rang Barton's garage to send help. I kept on trying and eventually it started and so I left a message with the man in the shop and went off on my round. He said, 'Don't worry, when I see the breakdown van, I'll tell them', but he obviously hadn't seen it because when I got back at night they went mad. Apparently they had sent a vehicle out

21

to look for me, with Derek and another driver. They had searched the area and couldn't find me, but Derek was delighted because he'd got an afternoon out from the garage.

I enjoyed driving out in the country, delivering bread and cakes to farms and country cottages. Only a few special customers got fancy cakes, which were kept in a little cupboard at the side, as rationing restricted how much we could make. I had my favourites and saved cakes for them in exchange for ham, bacon or eggs. We put in our orders each evening to collect the next morning, and we got a bill from the bakehouse for what we had taken. Once we had paid this, any profit we made was ours. If I had any plain buns left, I sold them to a friend of ours who had a shop, which suited us both. The buns cost a penny each and I sold them for twopence, which doesn't sound much, but when you got about seven dozen, it mounted up and was a nice addition to my basic wage of one pound a week. If ever there was a shortage of drivers, Derek would visit some of the RAF bases taking bread to the NAAFIs. He would also sometimes go up to Linton-on-Ouse at dusk to watch the bombers taking off.

G E Bartons (Courtesy of Hugh Murray)

I met a Canadian air gunner in the Burton Stone called Shep, and he went with me sometimes on my deliveries, if he wasn't flying. We were good friends and he had a terrific sense of humour. He was a great dancer and storyteller. He would stand in front of the fire at the Burton Stone and throw cigarettes over his shoulder. He always smoked Sweet Caporal, which were made from strong dark tobacco in thick square paper packets. Our cigarettes were not rationed but they were expensive and we could only get Turkish ones, ('Passing Cloud' brand which were oval in shape) and 'Turf' which tasted rather like manure. There was no Virginia tobacco imported from the States as Merchant Navy ships were only allowed to carry necessities. But Americans and Canadians got cigarettes from their PX stores. They seemed to have access to all sorts which the English could not get, goods which were slipped in amongst the more important things. Most people I knew smoked, as there was no suggestion that it might be harmful. All our favourite film stars smoked too, and once I'd seen Paul Henreid light two cigarettes for Bette Davis in 'Now Voyager' in 1942, I considered this the height of romance.

The clock at the Burton Stone was in the shape of a woman. The pointers were her legs and you could never tell what time it was because the guys were always moving them around. A friend of Shep's, another Canadian called Cy, would come on a brightly coloured bike and prop it up outside the De Grey Rooms. He was really kind, with a plumpish, lovely bright face, and would bring presents of eggs, fruit or chocolates, or something out of his parcels from home. He even had oranges and lemons on occasion, which were unheard of in English greengrocers, and endless packets of gum in his pockets. He always called me Jackson (which meant mate or buddy).

Once a friend of mine, Dennis, who lived in St Luke's Grove, off Lumley Road, had gone with me on the round and we were driving up Tadcaster Road. We could only use one side of the road as the other side was filled with stationary tanks and army vehicles parked ready for use. I had just signalled to turn left to a farm when I noticed a motor-bike which appeared to be trying to overtake me on the inside, because a car was coming the other way. As I turned, the dispatch-rider came right into the van and over the top onto the road. I got out and left the van, and Dennis and I walked up to the farmhouse to ring for an ambulance. When we got back there was nobody there - no man, no bike, nothing. When the police came they thought at first that I had made it up, but eventually believed me. We reckoned that an army truck had taken him away before the police arrived. I was glad I had reported it though because it had made a huge dent in the side of the van. There was no way that the man could have ridden the bike as the front wheel was completely bent, so someone must have picked him up.

I went to one farm regularly, where they had lots of geese and I was too terrified to get out, so I just tooted the horn and the farmer's wife came out to shoo them away whilst I got the bread out. They made an awful noise and were pretty fierce. Good 'guard' dogs!

I often went to a lovely little cottage in Aberford which was always spotlessly clean, with a highly polished red tile floor and clipped rugs they had made themselves. There was usually a lovely smell of baking and fresh food. They can't have had much because of the rationing, but they made it go a long way. The wife had four sons who all worked on the farm. They were really big men with big boots, and probably big appetites, and she was tiny, dwarfed by a large white pinny. It only looked as if it had two bedrooms upstairs as well as the two rooms downstairs, and I used to wonder where they all slept!

CHAPTER THREE
THE A.T.S.

On 15th September 1944, I returned to the ATS. The letter had arrived a
week before, enclosing my train ticket. Leaving my mother crying at the station
I set off, feeling both excited and nervous. I found I couldn't concentrate on the
book I had brought as my thoughts were too full. I sat watching trees, fields,
and houses fly by, not really seeing them. I tried not to remember the first time,
when I had been too young and too homesick to enjoy it. I told myself that I
was almost nineteen now, I was a woman.

Three hours later, I reached Leicester, and climbing out with my suitcase, I
spotted about a dozen girls standing together with an ATS sergeant. Feeling
sick in my stomach I sauntered over trying to appear relaxed, and the sergeant
asked my name. When I gave it, she looked down the list and ticked it off.
Some of the girls were already chatting to each other and I felt rather lost and
apprehensive until I heard someone say,

'Hello, how are you feeling? Isn't it exciting?'

'Actually I'm more scared than excited,' I admitted.

She introduced herself as Joyce and I told her my name was Alex. After
that we just stayed together and when the sergeant said a few minutes later,
'Right, we're all here, follow me,' we grabbed our suitcases and followed her to
the waiting army truck just outside the station. It was a bit difficult clambering
into the back of the lorry and we drove off feeling more like a herd of cattle
than human beings. The noise we made was not very different either.

Eventually we drove through the barrack gates, past barbed wire and sentry
boxes, amid a loud cheer from some young soldiers. The first few days were so
hectic that it was impossible to feel homesick. We had medicals, lectures, the
lengthy form filling as well as kitting out. The list seemed endless as we had to
pick three pairs of this, that and the other to put in our canvas kit bag. We were
measured and had to try on jackets, khaki shirts and skirts, brown ties,
stockings, tunics with a buckle on the belt and four pockets, and a brown cap
with the ATS badge. Then we had to sign for everything. There were brushes

for every possible purpose - hairbrush, clothes brush, shoe brush, button brush, button stick and a sewing kit (called a housewife) so we had no excuse not to look our very best. There was barely room for everything. The only storage space we had was a cupboard mounted on the wall above our beds. Joyce had the camp bed next to mine and we were glad of each other's company, talking into the night and getting to know each other better. The girls were a mixed bunch, from a variety of backgrounds, but we all seemed to hit it off reasonably, with only a few clashes of personality. There were a trio of characters who took to calling me 'Lady' because I was reserved and quiet in comparison to them, without much of an accent.

They were amused that I found it strange undressing in front of a roomful of women. It took time for some of us to adapt to sharing our lives and having no privacy. A few of the girls were used to sharing a room, but for me, communal living was quite a change.

This period was for training and we knew that after a month we would all be going our different ways, depending on which branch we had been assigned. We spent the first two weeks 'square-bashing', drilling on the square, learning to march in time. Left, right, left, right, quick march, with arms swinging. Then there was a period in the classroom, as well as PT in the gymnasium, which I wasn't very keen on, and cross country runs. We then had various trade tests, to decide where our skills and talents lay. Joyce and I were to be in transport, some girls would work on ack-ack guns, others as cooks, stewards or secretaries. At the end of the month we had a passing out parade, looking our smartest ready to march past the C.O. We were very proud by this time to feel a part of the British Army, ready to 'do our bit.' With buttons and shoes shining, we marched to the band and saluted by eyes right. I felt a lump in my throat and wanted to cry. We were all very different but, living together for four weeks, we had grown attached. In the evening was the farewell concert and then it was goodbye to lots of the girls.

Next day we packed our kit bags and Joyce and I set off for the Transport Corps in Camberley, where Princess Elizabeth (later to be Queen) also trained in 1945. Things were different at the new station, and instead of the day being fully organised for us, now we had to hang about a lot of the time. However after a day or two we soon settled in, and liked the routine of half day lectures and half day practical training. We were living in Nissen huts, with twelve beds in each, and the fire was the old iron type set in the middle, which was difficult to light. After a day's work we all huddled round it. We wore battledress and gaiters, hats, leather jerkins, coats, trousers and hobnail boots and we were certainly glad of them, as we walked through the woods to the bays where the vehicles were housed.

I was amazed how quickly I learned about the workings of an engine and how interesting I found it. We were all looking forward to getting out on convoy driving, and after some training in map reading, we were assigned in pairs to the army trucks, which were 15 hundredweight lorries. The first exercise was to send us out with a map, a given destination and a fixed time to reach it, taking any route we liked. We might just have time to call into a little cafe for tea and homemade scones.

Each night we had to drain the vehicle. In winter this was terrible because next morning we had to go to the line of trucks, find our own vehicle and there would be a pool of ice around it. This had to be defrosted with water, then before setting off we had to check the oil, petrol, water and the plugs. Even though the weather was hazardous, and our faces rarely seemed to be clean from working under the vehicles in our boiler suits, I was very happy.

There would be a signal which meant 'first away' and some of the lorries would set off after the dispatch rider and eventually we would all follow in a convoy. There were two of us in the vehicle, so that we could take turns in driving, sometimes at night. Once a week we had to change the wheels around, put the back ones where the front had been, so that they would wear evenly. There were no proper doors, just two pieces of glass for a windscreen and a canvas top. We were always frozen, and had to wear scarves over our hats and gauntlets over the top of the woollen gloves.

Halfway through the course we were given seven days' leave. We were all looking forward to going home, feeling very proud of ourselves in uniform with the transport wings, MT, on our arms. The great day came when we were fully

27

fledged drivers having passed all the tests. Only three disappointed ATS girls were sent back to be assigned to other trades as they were inadequate.

Joyce and I were lucky enough to be posted to London together and were sent to High Street Kensington. I loved being there, in the metropolis, though at first the size and busyness of it made me feel quite small. We had made other friends by now including two girls who had come together, Maureen and Pat, and soon the four of us were going out together whenever we had time off. We had to have a few trips around London with a corporal, to get the hang of driving in the capital and then were sent to the drivers' room where we were to report each morning. After a week of backseat driving, at last I was on my own. The first time was not a very thrilling errand, I was sent to another unit to collect spare parts. Yet to me it was a great accomplishment. The vehicle was a utility van called a Tilley with canvas at the back which rolled up. We had to transport machinery, plans or equipment around. It was essential to keep the Tilley clean, and in working order, so we had to understand vehicle maintenance. We had to take the rotor arm off when we stopped, to prevent anyone stealing it.

Pat and I had become very close friends, having the same sense of humour, and the same interests. We liked going to the Nuffield Centre (a British forces' club) or we might just go for a drink. We had an imaginary Scotch terrier which we used to take out with us and we would get people's attention by saying, 'Get under there Scotty' or 'Behave yourself boy'. When we ordered our drinks, we would ask for an ashtray to be filled with water for him. Everyone would look to see where the dog was. We made a lot of friends through this dog as it was a good way of breaking the ice. One night in a pub, a couple of women who were obviously looking for 'trade' were getting annoyed because they were being ignored, as we were causing great amusement with Scotty. After a bit, one of them came over and said, 'Will you take your bleedin' dog out, it's just peed up my leg.' Everyone shrieked!

One night we met some Americans and got invited to a dance at Rainbow Corner, a club for American forces run by the American Red Cross, which was on the corner of Piccadilly Circus and Shaftesbury Avenue. The food and entertainment there were superb and the atmosphere was terrific. You could get stuff that the English hadn't seen since before the war. We could only go in as the guests of Americans, and for them it was a home from home, open 24 hours a day with everything provided. Many of the volunteers were English, and they seemed to be willing to work round the clock, sewing, playing table tennis, cooking and a hundred other services. We couldn't get much make-up then, and once in the cloakroom at Rainbow Corner, we got into conversation with an American nurse who gave us a case full.

Alexina in the ATS

We loved going to the dances there which were held almost every night, and I remember listening to Connie Boswell and then taking doughnuts and coffee onto the roof to watch the searchlights over the city. You could see for miles. Once there was an air raid and the siren went but no-one moved, and the band kept on playing. We could hear the bangs of doodlebugs but we somehow didn't feel afraid. Everyone cheered. I saw Glenn Miller there twice which was the highlight of the year for me. I loved swing music, and dancing to such songs as 'In the Mood' and 'Moonlight Serenade.' We were devastated when we heard, not long afterwards, that Glenn Miller had gone missing over the

English Channel.

In one of the clubs I got to know a Canadian airman whose name was David. He would ring me when he was off duty and if I was free then we would meet. His mother was English and had married a Canadian soldier during the First World War, who had taken her back to his home in Saskatchewan. David told me that after the war he wanted to stay in England for a while to explore the places where his mother had been when she was young. Pat was also going out with an airman so we often went on double dates. David introduced me to drinking his favourite, rye and dry on the rocks.

One weekend we went to visit two of his aunts who kept a sweet-shop in Theydon Bois, a little village in Essex, two miles south of Epping, close to Waltham Abbey and bordered by the six thousand acres of Epping Forest. We got there by train direct from London. It is an area steeped in history and I was told that the forest had once been the hiding-place of Dick Turpin, as well as Queen Elizabeth's I's hunting ground. We arrived on Saturday afternoon and spent the evening talking to his aunts. After they had gone to bed we toasted marshmallows over a big fire. On Sunday we went for a long walk. It was such a pretty place, with a village green and pond in the centre, and to the west were lots of small coppices and woods. Nearby there were black fallow deer running wild, though we did not see any. We did see plenty of birds, including several robins, and other species I had never seen before. The woods and trees were covered with snow, and we crossed an old bridge over a little stream. We stood on the bridge for a while and David put my hands in his pocket to keep them warm. He told me then that he had fallen in love with me and I knew that I felt the same. He took off the signet ring he always wore and asked me to keep it.

His aunts were very kind and made me feel at home over the weekend. When we left, they filled my pockets with sweets and made me promise to visit them again. Soon after that weekend David went away and was posted abroad. We wrote to each other a few times and then there was a silence. Finally I had a letter from Theydon Bois, telling me that he had been killed. I cried and cried, it was my first really painful loss.

30

Life seemed to be very short, as every night there were air raids and the devastation was frightening. From June 1944 until the autumn it was the time when the buzz bombs were coming over. These were the V1 flying bombs, doodlebugs, or 'pilotless planes' as the newspapers called them. They flew in a straight line, and once the buzzing stopped we knew they were going to drop. They were operated by a gyro which kept them flying straight and level. They mostly fell in daylight and caused very high numbers of casualties. The Germans had begun a concentrated attack on the south of England with them and then they were superseded by the V2 rockets which were even more powerful.

For a while I was put onto driving ambulances. We had to reverse these big vehicles through narrow gates. When I drove I always had a medical orderly with me, and when we finished we were both exhausted. We sometimes went down into the underground, where hundreds of people were taking shelter. They arrived at dusk with rolled-up mattresses, or sleeping bags, thermos flasks, sandwiches, cases of belongings, and valuables. We would often have to climb over families having their supper. But I was touched by the spirit of comradeship, of people sharing with each other, talking, laughing and singing.

My time off varied and sometimes I worked all night and sank into bed worn out, as well as upset at some of the sights. Leave came one weekend a month and ten days every three months, but going home was like a different world, even though the war had affected everywhere. I met a French-Canadian in London called Jimmy. When I went home on leave, he asked for my address to write to me. I had only been home a day when he arrived on the doorstep asking to stay. He said he had slept in a field the previous night! We let him stay but he was a real pain and followed me everywhere like a lap-dog. He had no money either so had to be paid for when we went out. In any case, it wasn't easy for me to be interested in any man, for I compared them all to David.

One night Pat and I met a very tall, handsome naval officer on the tube, the Piccadilly Line. I don't know how we got into conversation with him but people just talked to each other on trains quite naturally. He asked us for a drink and we went to a really nice pub with a sedan chair which was a telephone kiosk,

31

then onto a club near Piccadilly where we had a meal. It got to 10.30 and we said we would have to go. He told us to ring in for a late pass. We said a late pass would only last until 11.59, but we might be able to get an all-night pass, even though it was against regulations, so he offered to book us into a hotel for bed and breakfast. We rang the duty officer, who we knew well, to request a pass and told her that we were staying the night with a cousin. We were very lucky that she agreed as we could have been reported AWOL. Overnight passes (usually for 48 hours) were like gold, and had to be applied for in advance.

At 2.30 in the morning we left the club and the officer took us to Adonino's where he booked us in for b and b, which cost five pounds each, and left us to get his train. We didn't get to bed until 3, and had to be up at 6, sleeping in our underwear as we had no other clothes with us, and no washing things, only the make-up we kept in our handbags. At 6 o'clock we rang room service and got coffee and toast in the bedroom, then raced back to camp. It had been a great night. All the girls wanted to know next day what had happened, and some didn't believe us. But it was true, he had been a Lieutenant Commander en route to Southampton, just looking for company on his last evening in England. Who knows what happened to him!

CHAPTER FOUR
BACK TO YORK

In 1945 I was given a compassionate transfer back to York as my mother had been ill and said she couldn't manage without me. The C.O. gave permission for me to live at home, and I found I had to share my room with Betty, one of the two ATS girls billeted on my parents. She worked for the Army Pay Corps in Bootham, at the top of Grosvenor Terrace, in an administrative post, dealing with soldiers' pay and accounts for the different depots. Half of the staff were civilians, including quite a few conscientious objectors, and the rest, like Betty, were military personnel. Soon she and I became good friends and often went out together.

I was a Driver 1st Class with F Company, York Garrison Group, working at Civilian Royal Engineers taking young men to the depots. Many of them were unable to be in the army for medical reasons. At first I worked down Water End where the vehicles were kept. I had to be able to wash and service my Tilley, to put it over a pit and clean the engine, use a grease-gun to oil the nipples underneath, then polish it until it was spick and span. I had learnt all the mechanics and maintenance side in Camberley and London. The vehicle always had to be in tip top condition ready for a call. If we broke down we could be put on a charge. We always had to look smart too and the shirts we wore had to be starched (at the Chinese Laundry) until the collar was stiff and gleaming. Whilst standing by, the three drivers sat in the driver's room writing letters and drinking tea, and other lads would come in for a natter.

Soon I was promoted to work at Fulford Barracks as a staff driver, which I enjoyed. I often drove the DMPS about (District Motor Power Superintendent) who was a colonel in a black limousine, and I also drove a couple of majors as well as several civilians, mainly architects. One day I had a captain who was very fond of himself and aware of his rank and kept criticising me in a patronising way, 'Driver, you're driving too fast...driver, you're driving too slow!' and so on. I got so sick of it that I pulled up and suggested he drove. It turned out that he didn't know how!

If we drove for more than four hours, we got a lunch allowance, and if we drove for more than eight hours we got a subsistence allowance of about 2/6 a day. One of the architects was great. I'd occasionally have to drive him for the whole day, and he would complete his business in the morning then take me to lunch and in the afternoon we would go to the pictures to make my time up to eight hours. Our pay was still not as high as the men's wages, so every penny helped. In London I had been paid 14 shillings a week, out of which I made an allowance of five shillings to my mother. The ATS also paid for our accommodation and clothes, with a small extra kit allowance. At the Barracks we had radio requests, and almost every day I would get a dedication from a captain for the Spike Jones song 'Cocktails for Two'. At first I was flattered, and even liked the song, but after three weeks I was sick of hearing it.

Sometimes Betty and I would go out for a drink with a body called Benny. He had a car and would sometimes let me drive. You would have thought I'd have enough of driving all day, but I loved driving all sorts of cars. One night we were coming back from Bishopthorpe and I asked if I could drive.
Then I spotted two boys in front who I knew, and decided to follow them. They were going quite fast and so I chased after them, tearing round corners and whizzing over kerbs. Benny was petrified and Betty was lying on the floor in the back, screaming, 'let me out, let me out.' Eventually we lost the boys and so we drove home. For some reason, Benny was not so keen to take us out after that! Next time I saw the boys I told them and they thought it was hilarious. Betty was supposed to wear glasses, but she hated them. One night she had gone off to meet an air force chap in Betty's Bar but arrived home in a state about an hour later. She had left her glasses behind, but then she couldn't see a thing, so she missed her date. After searching in vain, she left Betty's and then nearly got knocked down by a car in Davygate.

One night I met a Flight Lieutenant with a big silver Jag, which he would let me drive. I adored driving that car, and at first I enjoyed his company and liked the fact that girls would excuse me to dance with him, as he was very attractive. But he turned out to be a creep and later I heard that he was married. I had arranged to see him one evening but had forgotten that Betty and I also had a date with two army captains at the Olde White Swan in Goodramgate. When he turned up, Mother told him I was out, and before he had got into his car, our taxi arrived. Mother kept him talking while Betty got in and I had to run out of the back over the fields to Cromer Street where the taxi picked me up. I lay down on the floor of the cab in case he was still in the neighbourhood. Half an hour later we were in the White Swan when he walked in. He had seen me before I was able to hide, and he came over and said nastily, 'Thank you so much for keeping our date.' I pretended that I had forgotten all about it.

Betty and a friend

I now went to the De Grey Rooms to dances, often with Betty or Mary, another good friend who also worked at the Pay Corps. It was bigger than the Albany and held dances on Mondays, Wednesdays, Fridays and Saturdays. Tuesdays and Thursdays were for private functions including various charity balls which were often in aid of the Red Cross. The dances lasted from 7.30 to 12 and admission was 2/6. Two of the most popular bands were Bert Keech and his band, and Derek Dunning's band, who also played at swing dances at Clifton ballroom. I wore uniform most of the time because we hadn't enough coupons to buy many civvies, but it didn't seem to spoil my chances. Even in

35

battledress and boots I always got plenty of dances. The chaps were not allowed to wear civvies at night so they were always in uniform, and the RAF boys would be in battledress if they had just landed. Bert Keech ran the De Grey Rooms and late in the evening, he would stand in the doorway at the top of the stairs, turning away anyone who seemed the worse for wear with drink. There was a friendly rivalry between the British RAF and the Canadian airmen, who would delight in pinching each other's girls. They often continued their bantering down to Petergate fish and chip shop, where they bought bags of chips and proceeded to throw them at each other.

De Grey Rooms in the 1930s (Courtesy of Hugh Murray)

One night Mary, her boyfriend Jerry and I went to an officer's ball in Clifton. I wore a dress on this occasion and a set of bright red false nails. I was dancing with a young naval officer when I saw Molly come by with Jerry, gesticulating wildly. I hadn't a clue what was the matter, but then suddenly I noticed that my partner's shoulder had a nail stuck to it. I whispered to Molly as she came past, 'Can you retrieve it?' Jerry moved back and she managed to dance close enough to remove the offending nail. But when it came off, some of the pile was removed with it. Fortunately the officer was completely unaware of what was happening.

By this time Derek was at the North Eastern School of Wireless Telegraphy in Otley, training to become a radio officer in the Merchant Navy. He had received a letter on 13th January 1944 asking him to report as a cadet in six days. In that time he was expected to learn the Morse Code and obtain the HM Postmaster General's 'Handbook for W.T. Operators.' He enjoyed the course at Otley and would come home at weekends so we often went to dances together. We were very close and good company for each other. When he turned 18 in April 1945, he had to leave the wireless college and was sent into the army, in the Royal Signals.

At the De Grey Rooms, I met Johnny, who was a pianist in the RAF. He made a record of himself playing 'Beware my Foolish Heart' for me. But then he was posted abroad and I never heard from him any more. It was the case with so many of them, and we had to quickly learn to forget in order to cope with constant losses. Some nights we would go to the De Grey Rooms and a whole crowd of lads would be missing. They hadn't returned from a mission. I had made a vow not to get involved with anyone again, not to feel what I had felt for David. I enjoyed men's company but tried to avoid anything deeper. I had become friendly with Andre, a Belgian fighter pilot, stationed at Clifton (York) Aerodrome. He would always arrive late at night when he had been on missions, in his flying gear, and I'd be in my dressing gown about to go to bed. But I'd get dressed, and we would go off to dances in his sports car. He was shot down later. It was so hard to bear but we went on, almost able to switch off, and pretend it hadn't happened. It was the only alternative there was.

I was even more wary when something dreadful happened to Mary. She and Jerry had been very much in love, and then one night he proposed to her in the Burton Stone. She was over the moon, and talked of nothing else. A week later he too was dead. Our moods could fluctuate, moving quickly from anxiety and even despair, to optimism, trust and hope in the future, mingled with a fierce patriotism.

One of my good friends was Al Mercer, a wireless operator in the Royal Canadian Air Force, and a journalist in civvy street. He could always be relied on to cheer me up, had a great sense of humour and an excellent memory for amusing stories. I called him Big Feet Indeed, because he once trod on my toes at a dance and I accused him of having big feet, to which he replied, 'Big Feet Indeed.' He used to blink a lot, and a girl who came to tea with us, thought he was trying to get off with her, because he kept 'winking' at her all during tea.

One night Mary and I were at a pub in Fulford, when another friend's brother, Dinkie, flew in and told us that the motorised police were coming. The landlady had forgotten to ask for a drinks extension, and it was after hours so we had to hide. We ended up in a garage under a vintage car along with a senior police officer and his girlfriend. It was two o'clock when Dinkie came and told us to disperse in twos. We were all frozen and could not even get a hot drink. We called in again the next day and found out that they had left just after us, so we were lucky. We often seemed to get into scrapes and one night we got caught by MPs when we were getting a lift back from a dance in Church Fenton. Aircrew were usually able to get petrol but were only supposed to use it in a certain zone. York was too far from the camp, and we were stopped and all told to get out of the car. Fortunately they were let off with a warning, but it could have been more serious.

Another night, Mary, Betty and I were on our way to a dance at the officer's mess at Linton, when an air-raid started. We all ended up in a ditch which was full of water, and our evening dresses, the only ones we had, were very muddy. When the all-clear sounded, we sped off to the party and spent ages in the cloakroom trying to tidy ourselves up and wash off the mud!

Fortunately when we emerged it was quite dark. A whole crowd of airmen were sitting on the floor eating ham sandwiches, which looked very funny to us. A small squadron leader asked Mary to dance and when they sat down, his feet did not reach the floor. I couldn't stop laughing and Mary was trying desperately to keep a straight face. Then we were presented to the A.O.C., wishing that we weren't there. He knew us and gave such a big grin when he saw Mary's partner. Next day he rang her at the office and said, 'I see you're coming up in the world. Do you want a pair of stilts for your little friend?' which really embarrassed her, especially as all calls were recorded on the Northern Command tape.

CHAPTER FIVE
ENDINGS AND BEGINNINGS

By the beginning of May 1945, we knew that the end of the war was imminent. Plans were being made for VE Day, which was expected anytime. We heard that the Minster bells would ring for an hour as soon as peace came. On 2nd May, air raid warnings were discontinued and restrictions on torches were lifted, with vehicle lighting returning to peacetime regulations. The Civil Defence was also wound up.

By 5th May, Union Jack flags, streamers, bunting, hats and rosettes were on sale all over York market. Kids were collecting old furniture, mattresses and other rubbish, to build bonfires ready for the big moment. The VE celebrations began on Monday 7th May, when the ceasefire started, though hostilities officially ended at one minute past midnight. On VE Day itself, Tuesday the 8th, there were street parties all over York, with teas (trestle tables were assembled in the shape of a V), children's sports, games, races and fancy dress. In some areas, pianos were brought out into the streets and dancing went on into the night. The King's broadcast was relayed into Parliament Street by means of loudspeakers, and children followed the marching bands through town, dancing and waving flags.

On VE night, York really came alive. Betty and I went into the Burton Stone which was filled with RAF boys buying all sorts of mixed drinks. We had a few then decided to go on to a dance. There were victory dances at the Albany, the Co-op and the Clifton Ballroom, but as usual we preferred the De Grey Rooms. Bert Keech's band was playing there all week, and the atmosphere was electric. All the windows were flung open, and people were dancing out into the street. The pubs had extensions to 11.30 and the dance-halls to 1am. I was wearing uniform and ended up with half a tie, as some Canadians were going round clipping ties for keepsakes. We joined them and helped to collect various objects including a Keep Left sign and a top hat.

We spilled into Exhibition Square, arm in arm, singing every song we knew, when somebody suggested doing the conga round York Minster, which was floodlit from 10 o'clock. The bells had been ringing and the sound was magical. The lantern tower of All Saints' Church in High Ousegate was also illuminated, for the first time in 500 years! Many lights came on again, and people were lighting bonfires all over town, some burning effigies of Hitler. We hadn't been able to celebrate Bonfire Night since before the war, but now there were fireworks filling the sky with colour. In fact the last big celebrations in the city had been for George VI's coronation in 1937, which were a little spoiled by rain.

We seemed to see practically everyone we knew, and although I didn't see her, I heard that Connie and her family had been there, with her baby in a large pram. Her husband was still away in Africa (until 1946) and had never seen his daughter. People were grabbing us in the street, hugging and kissing us. It was an incredible feeling, nothing quite like it. There was an enormous sense of relief and joy and optimism. I guess we all believed that life was now going to be marvellous, that winning the war had changed everything for the better. Class distinction had seemed to disappear during the war, or at least go underground, for there was a lot of mutual sharing and help. The joy was overwhelming, but there was still the odd pang as I thought of David and John and Andre and others who would never see the peace they had longed for. It was after 5 am when we finally got home that night, and next day I found a pile of 'souvenirs' littering the living room.

The celebrations continued on VE Day Plus One, which was designated a public holiday, and there were some services of thanksgiving in various York churches. We were also promised a further holiday in September, which would be called VE Day 3. The following Sunday, the 13th May, was named Thanksgiving Sunday. There was a big parade of all York servicemen and women, Civil Defence, railway and other war workers. It was headed by the Royal Navy and the Wrens, then the Army (including 50 ATS from the York Garrison Group) were next, followed by the RAF, and then the various other groups. We assembled at St George's Field at 1.35, marched down Clifford Street, Coney Street, Lendal and Museum Street to the Minster for the service at 2.30 pm. Included in the hymns we sang was 'Rejoice O land in God thy might', which seemed particularly appropriate. Afterwards there was a march past in Deans Park, where the Princess Royal took the salute, then we continued via Blake Street to Parliament Street where we dispersed. There were a huge number both marching and watching, despite a cold and very wet day, and we felt proud to be a part of it.

We had expected, with the end of the war, that rationing would also cease, but it didn't. In fact we had to get our new ration books on May 28th from St Luke's parish hall on Burton Stone Lane. But petrol rationing ended on June 1st and over the Whit weekend and early summer, hundreds of York people flocked to the coast for the first time in years.

At the end of July, I came home one evening to find that Betty was meeting Leo, a twenty-three year old pilot in the RAF who was stationed at Full Sutton, eight miles from York. She had been seeing him for a few weeks though he had only been in Yorkshire since December 1944, and he had taken her to London the previous weekend to meet his parents, so things had become quite serious. She told me they would soon be engaged. I still hadn't met him as he had always been flying when I was at home, which wasn't often, but now she wanted me to make up a foursome with his friend.

I was quite tired that night but agreed to go as I knew Betty wanted to show him off. 'I know you'll love him,' she said, laughing. She could not have imagined what was to happen. As soon as I saw this man with the fair hair and laughing eyes, it really was love at first sight and I could tell by the way he was looking at me that he was aware of something between us. It was as if there were zigzags of electricity in the air. When he asked to dance with me, I refused at first as I didn't want to be alone with him. 'Go on, Alex, you know you love dancing,' Betty urged me, words which she would soon regret.

We danced together to the Vaughn Monroe song 'There I've said it Again,' and I felt the same electric charge as he held me close. When he asked if he could meet me, I told him that it wasn't possible. He was supposed to be crazy about my best friend!

41

It was an exhilarating though difficult evening. As soon as we got in, I went straight to bed, claiming to be very tired, leaving the others still talking downstairs. But it was a long time before I got to sleep, and I couldn't get him off my mind, feeling terribly guilty at the same time. The day after his return to camp I received a letter telling me that he had fallen for me. I steeled myself not to reply, though I desperately wanted to. Another letter arrived soon afterwards begging me to see him. I wrote back, explaining that whilst he was dating Betty I could not and would not get involved. Two days later he had broken it off with Betty and six weeks later Leo and I were married!

Alexina and Leo in Witney, September 1945

CHAPTER SIX
LEO'S WAR

Leo was born near Barnes in South London in 1922, and one of his favourite childhood memories was of being taken by his father down to Putney Bridge to watch the Boat Race. In the late 1920s the family moved to Heston near Hounslow, and Leo attended Spring Grove Secondary School in Isleworth, where his best subject was English. The nearby Spring Grove Central School had, as its headmaster, the author H.E. Bates.

On 21 July 1941, along with his best friend Bob, he enlisted in the Royal Air Force. They reported to the Air Crew Reception Centre at Lords Cricket Ground and for a few weeks lived in nearby flats in St John's Wood before being posted to Newquay Initial Training Wing in 'A' flight with No 1 squadron. This period was principally for study. Bill and Leo shared a room with a very serious-minded youth who spent most of his time working. He constantly complained at their frivolity and noisiness. One night the two of them came in at 2.30 am and instead of undressing for bed, changed the time on the clock to 6.30, started to rush about getting ready to leave, then woke up their room-mate telling him to hurry or he would be late for parade at 7. He woke in a panic, dashed around, shaved, washed and then when he had finished, they undressed and got into bed, much to his astonishment. He wasn't at all happy.

On 14th February 1942, they moved on to No 9 Elementary Flying Training School at Ansty near Coventry for a few hours dual flying and were then sorted out as potential pilots and sent to the Air Crew Dispersal Centre at Heaton Park, Manchester. Leo's first flight was on 16th February, just before his 20th birthday, in a DH 82 Tiger Moth.

In March they left for Gourock, near Glasgow, arriving at the port of embarkation at 6 in the morning, having travelled all night. They were ferried aboard the SS Banfora, which was in fact an ex-cattle boat, bound for Halifax in Nova Scotia, Canada. The ship was of French origin and make, registered at Marseilles; a vessel of 10,000 tons, about 27 years old and rather old-fashioned. One of the crew told them that it had been captured at Dakar by a British warship.

The sleeping accommodation was very crowded with many of the chaps in the hold of the ship with no portholes to provide fresh air and daylight. Leo and Bob slept in adjoining hammocks. The journey began with marvellous weather, so that the pair spent much of their time lounging in the sun on the promenade deck. Beer, sweets and chocolates were plentiful, and tins of fruit and condensed milk could be obtained, all of which were rationed at home. Cigarettes in the canteen were duty-free, with Players costing 4d for ten, and Woodbines only 3d. They were pre-war cigarettes with silver paper and cellophane wrappings, which were missing from British wartime brands.

Together with another boat filled with German aircrew prisoners of war, they were escorted by two destroyers across the Atlantic. Within three days of leaving, the roll had become quite considerable, and most of the human cargo were being very seasick. Bob, in fact, was the only one who wasn't sick. One night a hot water pipe burst in the mess and many of the men were soaked, especially those sleeping on the floor. The same evening a submarine had been reported in the vicinity, which added to the panic. The weather became increasingly worse and most of the men were lying about the decks constantly being sick and looking as white as ghosts. The waves were sometimes as high as twenty feet.

A sweep was started to guess the time of arrival. For 6d entrance fee, the winnings would be 50 pounds. As the storms lessened, the men returned to normal and became much livelier, playing pontoon or taking the air on deck. Every few days, they had to put clocks and watches back one hour. It took fourteen days to zig-zag across the Ocean, punctuated by several more submarine alerts.

From Halifax they boarded a giant Canadian locomotive to Moncton, almost on the boundary of Nova Scotia and New Brunswick. The weather was much better and the scenery beautiful. Their first impressions of Canada were favourable ones. There was no blackout, and the blazing light from shop windows filled with oranges and chocolates and almost every kind of article at fairly reasonable prices, was a fantastic sight. Each night the gang went out to have a supper of steak, hamburger or eggs, at the grills which stayed open until 2am. Even meals in the transit camp were amazing, compared to those back

44

home. There were eggs a-plenty, as well as bowls of butter, sugar and jam on the table.

There was a system at the YMCA where local citizens volunteered to 'play host' to the airmen, who picked out a couple of names from the list, to visit for meals and hospitality. After a month at the New Brunswick transit camp, they boarded a train for Florida via New York and Boston where they changed trains, spending a day at each. Leaving the train at New York's Pennsylvania Station, they managed to see something of the city, including the Waldorf Astoria, Broadway, The Bowery, Times Square and Jack Dempsey's. They eventually arrived at No 5 British Flying Training School, at Clewiston in Florida, a small town in the Sugar Bowl of the USA, at the southern tip of Lake Okechobi, just north of the Everglades, and 90 miles from Miami and West Palm Beach. They were encountered by temperatures in the nineties, palms and orange groves.

Leo and Bob and the others on Course 8 were instructed in the art of flying by US civilians at Riddle McKay Aero College. They flew primary trainers (PT17 Stearman biplanes) for the first three months, with night flying and aerobatics in the third month. In August they moved onto basic (BT 13A Vultee monoplanes) and finally on September 29th, to advanced training aircraft, which were AT 6A Harvard monoplanes. The Americans always referred to their aircraft by letters and numbers. Leo's first solo flight took place on 21st May in a PT17. There was also link training, in simulated flying machines on the ground. This gave extra tuition in instrument flying, and trained the cadets to rely on their instruments.

The course ended with a 2000 mile cross-country flight from Clewiston to Tennessee. Leo graduated from the flying school on 11 November, with all the usual American razzamatazz, and along with his 'wings' was also presented with a bracelet, inscribed 'Best Ground School Cadet.'

Whilst in Florida they had a wonderful time, and the hospitality shown by the Americans was amazing. This was not long after Pearl Harbour and the Americans had become very patriotic and very pro-British. Every weekend the cadets were taken into Miami or Palm Beach to be entertained. They visited the

Roney-Plaza Cabana Club, the Seminole, Hotel Metropole and the Deauville Hotel in Miami Beach. Another favourite place was Zissons Bowery where the food and entertainment were excellent, the latter still good at 4 am. They would also visit the Dixie Crystal Cinema in Clewiston, and the swimming pools were very well used. The tennis player Donald Budge came to the camp to coach the men, and Leo became quite a reasonable player.

Leo in Miami 1942

Leo and Bob got to know a family in Fort Lauderdale and would go to stay in their bungalow at the weekends. They were picked up at the camp, driven around and entertained for two days and then taken back on the Sunday night. The boys also stayed at the Clewiston Inn where they tasted alligator tail as a starter! The hotel had special rates for air cadets and the service was very friendly. They occasionally attended services at Clewiston church, and on going through the doors, were handed a hymn book and a paper fan, to combat the intense heat!

During the course, they were given two weeks' leave and Leo, Bob and another friend, Lew, all being keen travellers, decided to hitchhike round the Gulf of Mexico to New Orleans, approximately 1000 miles. They took lots of

46

photographs on this trip. Films were easily available in the US, whereas in Britain they were unobtainable, except to official photographers. Leo was interested in historical buildings and in churches, and on the trip they visited quite a few, including a couple of the deep south Black gospel ones.

Leo (in centre) and fellow cadets with PT 17 in Clewiston

During this time they were plagued by the drunken exploits of one of their room-mates who would arrive back in the early hours, make lots of noise and finally fall asleep in a drunken stupor. The nights were warm, and on one such, Leo and Bob and two others completely lifted this man's bed, in which he was snoring in a deep sleep, and carried it out of the room into the middle of an adjoining playing field, without waking him. They were all awakened early next morning by a naked figure bursting into the room asking for assistance to get his bed back. They had overlooked the fact that he slept in the nude and all his clothes were still over a chair in the room! Leo was well-known for his practical jokes, but no-one could be angry with him for long as he had a charm that was irresistible. Once at Full Sutton, someone retaliated to a fairly mild prank, by putting a so-called 'tame' white rat into Leo's bed. It was quite a dangerous thing to do as rats are almost impossible to tame, and Leo was not too pleased!

Back in England, the new graduates had to undergo a selection process, with psychology tests and other exams to discover their particular skills and potential. Leo spent two months at the Pilot's Reception Centre in Harrogate, where he was chosen for multi-engined aircraft. Bob, on the other hand, was assigned to single-engined fighters and went on to fly Spitfires. After a month at No 11 Elementary Flying Training School in Perth, Leo moved back to Harrogate and then on for another month to No 5 Pilots' Advanced Flying Unit at Ternhill in Staffordshire flying Ansons, and Master I and III aircraft. From there he spent a short time in Shobden, and eleven months in GTS Stoke Orchard flying Hotspur gliders, then towing them with Master aircraft. As a tug pilot he was assessed as 'above average.' By March 1944 he was in South Cerney for two weeks, then moved on to training on Oxfords with 1539 B.A.T. flight in Bibury.

Bob, Dennis, Leo, and, seated, Lew. Miami 1942

It was at the Operational Training Unit in Kinloss where he formed his crew in June 1944. After two weeks in the classroom they began training on Whitley V aircraft as a preparation for the Halifax. During these weeks, the men got to know each other and the pilots would choose their crews. The crews then moved to Acaster Malbis Air Crew training school for a few weeks, and in September to the HCU (Heavy Conversion Unit) at Riccall, to train on Halifaxes. The flight engineer joined the crew there, making up the complement of seven, and they were posted to 77 Squadron, part of 4 Group, at Full Sutton, in November 1944. Squadron personnel were continually changing, many crews finished their tour of ops and then moved on, whilst others were lost in action. In between each operation, some of the men were quiet, withdrawn, and introverted, perhaps reliving the trauma of their missions. Leo was very lively and cheerful, always joking and playing tricks. It was perhaps a way of coping, but was also his natural character. At the same time he was deep and sensitive and serious when he needed to be.

He formed a close friendship with Ron, another pilot who joined the squadron at the same time. They always sat together for briefings, and could often be found pouring over pilot's notes together. They shared a friendly rivalry as each raced towards the '30' mark. 30 ops meant the tour was finished and there would be a period away from it all. Ron did make it, just before VE Day, but Leo had only completed 27 ops and three early returns which did not count, so he did not qualify for leave and was required to stay with the squadron as it changed to Transport Command.

The squadron, in common with others, had a 'line-shoot' book in the flight office, and if any officer boasted or 'shot a line', it was entered in the book by a witness and a fine of 6d had to be paid. This went into a fund to take out the ground crews. Leo and Ron (or Flash and Joe as they called each other) would seize every opportunity to score points off each other and enter such 'lines' as Leo's, 'I never overshoot unless told to by control', and Ron's line, 'I've been on this squadron so long I know everybody by sight.'

CHAPTER SEVEN
LEO AND I

As soon as Leo and I got together, we wanted to be with each other as much as possible, and hated to be apart. Even when he was flying he would send me messages. Sometimes at Lumley Road, I could hear the roar of planes flying overhead. I would run outside and see one aircraft suddenly dip its wings and I knew it was his.

I started going to parties and dances at Full Sutton with Leo and soon got to know his crew, who were all nice, friendly guys. Fortunately my friendship with Betty was, after initial difficulties, not affected by my relationship with Leo. In fact we remained very close for the rest of Betty's life. She soon became involved with someone else and later met up again with Allan Farrar, the airman who drove a converted hearse, and they were married. After the war he became a pilot with Dan Air, flying the old York aeroplanes.

Leo's crew were very proud of their 'skipper'. One of them, Johnny, told me how much they relied on him. They were shot up badly twice. Once they were over France and had the choice to get home or to bale out as fuel was very low. Leo wouldn't think of baling out so the others stayed with him. They just made it over the Kent coast and as they touched down, the engine began to stall. There had been just enough fuel to get that far. The navigator told me that he hardly ever looked out of the window because the first time he did, he saw two planes crashing in mid-air above Heligoland. He didn't envy the pilot who had to fly through the constant flak and gunfire. They were hit a few times and had to land in other parts of England but they always made it back somehow. Although all the squadron members were on friendly terms, joining in the fun, laughing and drinking together, it was only really crews who formed deeper relationships. This was probably because they did not want to be too deeply affected by the constant losses, but Leo told me that spending so many hours together, in a confined area, in a dangerous situation, meant that a crew forged a special bond. There had to be a strong mutual trust if they were going to survive. For the pilot in particular, the responsibility was very great, as he knew that the others depended on him.

50

It was the weekend of VJ night (August 15th) when Leo took me down to London to meet his parents and tell them of our engagement. On the Friday night I waited at the end of the road whilst he broke the news. I was nervous, not knowing how they would receive me, especially after meeting Betty so recently. I had planned to spend the night in a nearby hotel but they asked me to stay at their house. Next day we went to buy the ring in Hounslow.

In June 1945 the squadron had transferred to Transport Command and converted to Dakotas. In August there was a huge farewell party and dance at the base. There were all sorts of events and sports during the day and in the evening the hangars were floodlit and decorated for the dance. The bands of both the RAF and the Free French Air Force from Elvington played into the night.

Leo and his crew

At the beginning of September, Leo and his crew moved to Broadwell. We were on the top of a bus when he told me he would soon be leaving for India, and then suggested that we get married before he went. Their departure was set for the 25th September, so a few days before that, we went down to the registry office at Witney near Oxford and were married there. We told no-one except my mother, sending telegrams to my Dad and to Leo's parents! His wireless op was our best man and the registrar's daughter our other witness, and we had photographs taken outside the parish church. On the register I had put down my age as 21 instead of 19 (so that we did not need parental consent) and when we got back to the hotel we were trying to change it without it looking obvious, feeling guilty and giggling like children. My Dad and Leo's parents were furious but there was nothing they could do. When Dad realised that it was what I wanted, he soon came round, and so did Leo's father. His mother was a very different proposition. Funnily enough, Ron, Leo's pilot friend from 77 squadron, also got married the same week as we did, though neither of the men knew about that until later. Some people thought that their competitiveness even extended into their private lives!

From Broadwell, Leo flew to the Middle East (Sardinia, Syrenaica, Palestine, Sudan, Aden) and India. He was out there for seven months, stationed in Mauripur, near Karachi, and I didn't see him again until the following May but he wrote almost every day, long, intimate letters telling me about life in India! He had to number the letters as they arrived at different times, and I might get a batch all at once. He had bought the 78 rpm record of 'There I've said it Again' (which had become 'our song') and told me that every time he heard it, it reminded him of me. He drove the other guys mad playing it constantly until it was practically worn out. I continued to live with my parents and had a good time, the best of both worlds I suppose. I was married, with a certain status, yet still experiencing the same freedom I had known in wartime. My friends were quite envious.

When Leo got home he told me more about his experiences! On one trip Leo suddenly decided that he wanted to fly over the Taj Mahal at Agra, as it was one of the world's 'wonders'. They were nowhere near Agra and should not have been, but they made the trip and the crew got a look at the famous place, even managing to take an aerial photograph. Leo told Cyril, his wireless op, to give the base a false reading of their position, which would have meant serious trouble if they had been found out. They had to keep ground control informed of their whereabouts at all times.

In Broadwell, the squadron had trained in the towing of gliders, learning to snatch them off the ground. The Horsa glider would be on the runway with a tow rope, which was fastened on to a clothes line between two poles. The aircraft flew down with a hook on the arm, which picked up the glider. There was a drum within the aircraft and the minute the two engaged, and the tow-rope was taut, the drum would unwind so that there was no full force. As the aircraft and glider became airborne, the drum would wind in.

This exercise was necessary for their time in the Far East. A lot of glider pilots had been working in Burma and were waiting in Kargi Road. The 77 squadron pilots amongst others, picked up large numbers of army personnel near Calcutta, which was close to Burma, and flew them to Mauripur. A lot of converted bombers such as Yorks, Stirlings and Liberators then flew them home.

Leo had been in hospital for a short time at a small place out in the desert area, several miles from Karachi. When he came out, he had to join the other pilots in doing a certain amount of training. However experienced they might be, there were always more circuits and bumps and single-engine flying. He and Cyril went up in the aircraft and Leo decided to fly over the hospital, which he did three times at quite low level. When they landed, they were called in by the C.O. and questioned about it. They denied any knowledge of the incident! Another aircraft had also been flying in the same vicinity and the hospital did not get the aircraft letters so nothing could be proved and the squadron leader was unable to do anything about it. If they had been found out, it would have meant a court martial and probably being grounded for a few weeks.

Yet despite his penchant for playing tricks, Leo was very good at his job. In March 1946 he received a special commendation from the C.O. for having flown 250 hours without an accident, under the difficult conditions peculiar to South East Asia.

One morning when Leo and Cyril came to their briefing, they were told that an aircraft had gone missing. Six aircraft had flown out at 4am, across to Delhi and Calcutta, but only five had returned. The men asked, 'What do you mean there's an aircraft missing, the war's over?' But an SOS had been picked up, strangely enough, in Malta and relayed to India. Leo's crew were the first to be airborne to look for the missing aircraft, and set out following the route.

After an hour they picked up a message from Char, where there was an emergency landing strip, often used by Hurricanes. They assumed that the aircraft had made a false landing there, but a few minutes later they saw a Dakota on the ground with one wing broken.

They dropped their height and circled above it and were able to make contact with the other radio operator. They were quite near to a railway line so they told the other crew to make their way there. Leo landed at Char and went into the station to ask them to stop the trains. When the other crew arrived, he and Cyril organised a bullock cart and got all the crew's luggage onto it. While the men walked back along the track to the air strip, Leo and Cyril had to drive the bullock cart through the village, to make sure the luggage did not get lost.

On 5th October 1945 I left the ATS, though remained on the official list until April 1951. In the event of another war, drivers would be amongst the first to be recalled to duty. When Leo was demobbed from the RAF in July 1946, we stayed in York briefly then went to live in London, where he got a job as a Clerical Officer with London County Council. I started work at Fortnum and Mason, the large store near St James's Church, in Piccadilly, initially just serving customers, but then I did some modelling in their clothes department. We had bought a Ford Popular and visited a few places to which I had never been, including Runnymede where King John signed the Magna Carta in 1215.

Leo and Alexina in Heston 1946

We moved back to York in 1947 when I became pregnant. Derek came home on demob leave, which was lovely as it was the first time we had spent together in years. In February 1945 whilst waiting to go into the army, Derek had worked as a delivery van driver for S. Border and Sons, of 48 Coney Street, the high class grocers and Italian wine merchants, who also had a cafe on the premises. The entrance to the garage was opposite the Tower Cinema in New Street. They also employed errand boys who rode bicycles with huge baskets. In May 1947 after being demobbed from the Royal Signals, Derek returned to Borders.

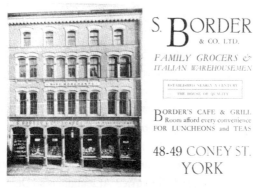

S Border & Son (Courtesy of Hugh Murray)

Leo transferred to work for the Council in York, and spent some time collecting rents. Derek would be out delivering groceries and so they arranged to meet up. Sometimes Derek would take his own motor bike, a 350cc BSA Empire Star. With Leo on the back, he rode out to Full Sutton aerodrome, now disused, and they would roar up and down the old runway where Leo had once taken off to fly over Germany. Derek had bought the bike when he was in the army in 1946, and as it was an ex-army model and all khaki, he stripped it down and painted it. BSA sent him the colour scheme and the logo transfers.

Two army friends came to York from a transit camp at Thirsk, and he took them both back on the bike. He was on the tank with the other two behind! They had all been to the fair in St George's Field first and had a few drinks! He finally sold that bike to a teacher in mid-1947 when petrol rationing was re-introduced.

Derek went back to wireless college in Cardiff from September to December 1947, to study for the Second Class PMG Certificate in Wireless Telegraphy. Once he had passed the exam, he returned to York and worked as a builder's labourer on the new extension to Lumley Barracks but after a week he and another man got the sack. Each time it started to rain they took shelter in the hut and made tea, and the foreman would storm in and say, 'I'll tell you when to shelter.' One day they had to dig a six-foot deep trench and there were no machines at that time to make it easier. When they thought it was deep enough, they sat down for a rest, and the foreman came over saying, 'I have a workman aged 60 who can do the same amount of work as both of you put together, and doesn't skive either!'

In July 1948 Derek went to sea on a P & O passenger ship bound for Australia. He was moved to another ship at Bombay on the way back so didn't get home until 1951! He had been corresponding for a while with Sadie, a girl who lived in South Wales, and eventually met her for the first time outside Cardiff station in November 1951, before setting off again from Cardiff on a coal freighter to Buenos Aires. There he spent a few days at the villa of our uncle who had emigrated to Argentina before the First World War to work on the railways. His children had all married Argentinians so Derek had the chance to meet lots of cousins and their families for the first time. When he got back to Cardiff, he married Sadie not long before he had to set off on another voyage to the West Indies and Rio with more coal.

Derek on the BSA motorbike. 1946

My first child, Michael, was born in August 1947, at Lumley Road. It had been a warm summer so I could enjoy sitting out in the garden. Afterwards Leo and I temporarily rented a very small house near to the railway in Field View, off Burton Stone Lane. Then we moved into a flat off St John Street, but I wasn't really very happy there, and felt lonely with just a small child for company. The sudden change from work and socialising and having a lot of freedom was a difficult hurdle for me. I was soon pregnant again and quite ill this time. In the summer of 1948 I woke one morning with violent pains. I was alone and had no telephone. At 2 o'clock my father popped in unexpectedly, which was very fortunate. I had already lost the baby and Dad was wonderful, calling the doctor and looking after me until Leo got home.

Although the war had been an awful time, with dreadful losses and the pains of parting with loved ones, it was also, particularly for women, a time of opportunities, of a freedom which we hadn't known before. The sense of mutual danger had brought the country close, had meant that people forged friendships more easily and were not afraid to speak their true feelings, knowing that tomorrow may be too late. When it ended we enjoyed the Victory celebrations and were happy that the killing was over. Yet there was also a sense of anti-climax, life became lonely and hard. Women were not considered so important anymore. They were expected to go back to being obedient little housewives and mothers, give the jobs back to the men, and adapt again to a different world. We felt isolated and unhappy a lot of the time. Although I loved Leo and Mike, I longed for the independence I had known during the war.

I wasn't the only one. In May 1948 Leo returned part-time to the RAF Volunteer Reserve, and did more training at the Reserve Flying School in Doncaster, back on Tiger Moths, then in July 1949 went to No 8 Elementary Flying Training School at Woodley, also flying on Chipmunks. He met up again with Cyril and later Bob, his friend from school and Florida days. When Leo wasn't flying, he wasn't really fulfilled. The lack of excitement, and difficulties in adapting to civilian life, influenced many flyers to return on weekends and during the summer holidays. Leo told me that flying was like a drug, without it they suffered withdrawal symptoms. The aircraft became a part of you, as if you yourself were flying, like the feeling when you run, ride a horse or drive a car, but much more exhilarating. In the early 1950s all these 'weekend flyers' were called up full time into the RAF, as things were hotting up in Korea. Some had to sign on for three months, and others, including Leo, for 18 months. I knew that he was delighted. In April 1952, he was given a post as training instructor and sent to South Cerney in Gloucestershire. We knew that after he had completed a few months' service we would qualify for a house and would be able to settle down in one place as a proper family. I was pregnant again and looking forward to a new start.

So Leo went off to Gloucestershire and I stayed at Lumley Road with Mike and my parents, awaiting the birth of my second child. But the new beginning was never to be, for on 28th July a telegram arrived to say that Leo had been killed in a mid-air collision between two Harvards over Ampney Down near Cirencester in the Cotswolds. There were two pilots in each aircraft, and they were on an exercise, 'flying blind', by their instruments alone. The cockpits were covered by canvas hoods, and as they began to climb on opposite courses, they were unaware of each other. All four were killed instantly.

Leo's funeral at South Cerney

The RAF gave the pilots a full military funeral on 31st July and they were buried in South Cerney churchyard. It was a terrible time and Leo's mother blamed me for allowing him to go back into the RAF and leave a safe but very dull job with the Council. It seemed so cruel, just when life was beginning to work out for us. My father went with me to the inquest and the funeral and was a marvellous support.

Two months after Leo's death, our daughter was born.

Alexina with her son and daughter

THIS BOOK IS DEDICATED TO
ALEXINA AND LEO,
MY PARENTS